SPOTLIGHT ON SOCIAL AND EMOTIONAL LEARNING

SPEAKING WITH PURPOSE

COMMUNICATION

JILL KEPPELER

PowerKiDS press.

NEW YORK

Published in 2020 by The Rosen Publishing Group, Inc.
29 East 21st Street, New York, NY 10010

Editor: Rachel Gintner
Designer: Michael Flynn

Photo Credits: Cover Hill Street Studios LLC/DigitalVision/Getty Images; cover, pp. 1, 3–4, 6–8, 10–12, 14, 16, 18–20, 22–24 (background) TairA/Shutterstock.com; p. 5 Syda Productions/Shutterstock.com; p. 6 Rick Friedman/Corbis Historical/Getty Images; p. 7 encierro/Shutterstock.com; p. 9 s_bukley/Shutterstock.com; p. 10 Studio 1One/Shutterstock.com; p. 11 Aaron Amat/Shutterstock.com; p. 12 Littlekidmoment/Shutterstock.com; p. 13 Mike Harrington/The Image Bank/Getty Images; p. 15 PeopleImages/DigitalVision/Getty Images; p. 16 marekuliasz/Shutterstock.com; p. 17 Everett Historical/Shutterstock.com; p. 18 LightField Studios/Shutterstock.com; p. 19 Pressmaster/Shutterstock.com; p. 21 Debby Wong/Shutterstock.com; p. 22 pathdoc/Shutterstock.com.

Cataloging-in-Publication Data

Names: Keppeler, Jill.
Title: Speaking with purpose: communication / Jill Keppeler.
Description: New York : PowerKids Press, 2020. | Series: Spotlight on social and emotional learning | Includes glossary and index.
Identifiers: ISBN 9781725306899 (pbk.) | ISBN 9781725306929 (library bound) | ISBN 9781725306905 (6pack)
Subjects: LCSH: Interpersonal communication--Juvenile literature. | Communication--Juvenile literature.
Classification: LCC BF637.C45 K377 2020 | DDC 302.2--dc23

Manufactured in the United States of America

CPSIA Compliance Information: Batch #CWPK20. For further information contact Rosen Publishing, New York, New York at 1-800-237-9932.

CONTENTS

EXPRESSING THOUGHTS, SHARING IDEAS 4
BUILDING BRIDGES 6
WRITTEN, SPOKEN, SIGNED 8
BODY LANGUAGE 10
COMMUNICATION SKILLS 12
BEING UNDERSTOOD 14
RESPECTFUL SHARING 16
HONE YOUR SKILLS 18
IF YOU'RE HAVING TROUBLE 20
COMMUNICATE! 22
GLOSSARY 23
INDEX 24
PRIMARY SOURCE LIST 24
WEBSITES 24

CHAPTER ONE

EXPRESSING THOUGHTS, SHARING IDEAS

When you think of effective communication, you might imagine a serious **conversation** between two adults, a formal letter, or a speech given by someone important. However, you communicate all the time—even when you don't realize it! Communicating means sharing knowledge or feelings. You can do this through spoken words, through writing, or through gestures or motions, just to name a few ways.

You communicate when you answer a teacher's question at school, when you write a "thank you" note to a relative, and when you shrug when your mom asks if you did your homework. You also communicate when you post something to social media, when you send a message to a friend asking her to play video games, and even when you argue with your brothers or sisters. People communicate in many different ways and styles. Some ways are more effective than others.

Raising your hand in class when you want to ask something or answer a question is communicating, too. It communicates that you want to speak.

CHAPTER TWO

BUILDING BRIDGES

Communication is how we make connections with other people. We communicate to get the things we need to live and to get **information**. Communication is a two-way process, however. We also communicate to share feelings and ideas. Listening can be just as important as talking when it comes to **verbal** communication. People communicate in different ways depending on their age and background. It's important to keep this in mind.

Alex, an African gray parrot, is shown in 2004 with professor Irene Pepperberg. Alex learned about 150 words and knew all his colors and shapes.

Animals communicate, too. They interact with other animals and with people. A dog's growl is a warning—so is a rattlesnake's rattle. A cat purrs to show it's content. Elephants twist their trunks together to greet each other. Can you think of other ways animals communicate?

Humans communicate with animals as well. Sometimes people teach animals hand signals. Sometimes animals learn to understand—or even speak—human words!

CHAPTER THREE

WRITTEN, SPOKEN, SIGNED

People often communicate in spoken words. There are more than 6,500 languages spoken in countries throughout the world! No one's absolutely sure how many there are in total. More people speak Mandarin Chinese than any other language, followed by Spanish and English. You and your friends and family members may speak more than one language. Some languages have a lot in common. Others don't!

Not every language has a written form. People who study languages think that about 4,000 languages have a writing system. There are many different alphabets used, too! Not every language uses the same letters we do.

There also are sign languages, including American Sign Language (ASL), British Sign Language (BSL), and many more. Sign languages have their own **grammar** and rules. You can have an **accent** in sign language just like you can while speaking aloud.

Actress and Academy Award winner Marlee Matlin sometimes uses ASL to communicate. She's acted in many movies and TV shows and has a star on the Hollywood Walk of Fame.

CHAPTER FOUR

BODY LANGUAGE

When you communicate with others, you not only share thoughts and feelings through words but also through body language. This means the way you move or gesture. Body language isn't just the movement of your hands. It also includes the movements of your face and your entire body. Sometimes body language can **contradict** what someone's saying. What would you think if someone tells you they're pleased to meet you, but while they speak, they're frowning at you? You wouldn't know what to believe: their words or their **expression**.

To communicate effectively, you need to keep your body language in mind. Try to be sure you're sending the message you're meaning to send. For example, if you want to be sure someone knows you're happy to see them, a sincere smile that involves your eyes as well as your mouth would help!

CHAPTER FIVE

COMMUNICATION SKILLS

There are many ways you can work toward communicating more effectively and clearly. When it comes to verbal communication, it's important to speak as clearly as you can. Keep your hands away from your mouth, and try not to mumble. Don't whisper, but don't yell either. It's no fun getting yelled at, and yelling at someone isn't a helpful way to communicate.

Usually, a common and polite way to communicate is to make eye contact with someone as you're talking to or listening to them. This shows you're paying attention and you're interested in what they're saying. Try not to stare too hard, though. If the person you're talking to looks uncomfortable, maybe you need to back off a little. Always keep in mind to whom you're speaking. You probably wouldn't talk to someone you just met the same way you'd talk to your best friend.

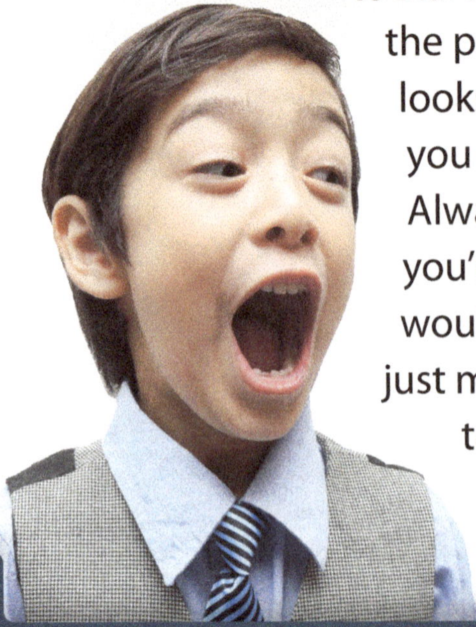

Speak up so people can hear you, but don't yell! Pay attention to other people's reactions.

CHAPTER SIX

BEING UNDERSTOOD

It's also important to be sure the person you're talking to can understand you. This can mean speaking clearly and not rushing through your words. It can also mean using good grammar and pronouncing your words correctly. Grammar rules exist, in part, to make sure we can understand each other effectively and with as little confusion as possible. This is true for spoken, written, and signed communication!

Make sure the words you use will be understood by the person or people you're talking to. You might use **slang** from your favorite video game when talking with your friends, but would you use it with your teacher? Maybe you would if the teacher also likes the game! But another teacher might not understand you. If you're talking to someone much younger, be careful not to use **complicated** words they haven't learned yet.

When you're speaking in front of a group, it's even more important to make sure you speak clearly. Make sure everyone can hear you.

CHAPTER SEVEN

RESPECTFUL SHARING

Good communication doesn't go in just one direction. It's important to listen when you're having a conversation with someone. Good communicators take turns speaking and listening. Don't interrupt the person who's talking, and don't interrupt someone to jump into a conversation between other people. If someone tells you something you don't quite understand, ask questions and listen to the answers until you do understand.

One good way to make sure you understand what another person is trying to tell you is to wait until they're done. Then, **summarize** what you think they've said and say it back to them. Ask, "Is that right?" If you misunderstood something, you'll find out. You can ask more questions until you do understand. This is better than standing there after the conversation and wondering what, exactly, you were talking about!

John Marshall, who was born in 1755 and served as the fourth chief justice of the United States, once said, "To listen well is as powerful a means of communication and **influence** as to talk well." As chief justice, Marshall probably knew a lot about both listening and talking.

CHAPTER EIGHT

HONE YOUR SKILLS

It's not always easy to communicate effectively. Some people are more social than others. They like to talk to other people, and this practice can help make them good communicators! Still, even if you're a little shy and don't like to talk as much, you can practice to **hone** your communication skills.

You could also work on improving your communication with your brothers or sisters—although they might wonder what you're up to!

Is there someone you do like to talk to? Are you more comfortable talking to adults or family members? Try starting conversations. Ask your mom or dad what they did at work that day. Listen to the answer, then ask more questions or tell them about your day. Be sure to wait until a time when they're not really busy with something else, though! Whether you're a kid or an adult, it's much tougher to communicate well when you're **distracted**.

CHAPTER NINE

IF YOU'RE HAVING TROUBLE

Even with practice, however, communication can be tough. You might not be able to think of what you want to say. You might not understand the other person very well for some reason. Be patient with yourself and others. Try slowing down and looking for ways to solve the problem.

Sometimes, people are better at speaking their thoughts than writing them out. Others, however, are much better at written communication than they are at spoken communication. They can explain things better and think of the right words when they have a chance to write them out. There's nothing wrong with this! If you feel this way, try sitting down and writing out what you want to communicate. This can help you better **articulate** the words you want to say. Then, you can keep what you wrote in mind when you need to speak about it.

John Green, the author of *The Fault in Our Stars* and many other books, once said, "Writing is something you do alone. It's a profession for (people) who want to tell you a story but don't want to make eye contact while doing it." Do you think this is true?

PAPER
PUR COUTURE
SAINT LAURENT

CHAPTER TEN

COMMUNICATE!

From the time we're babies, we're trying to communicate with those around us. We go from crying or making faces to convey what we're feeling to learning to talk, write, and express our thoughts and emotions. It's not always easy, but with good communication skills, patience, and practice, we can get better at connecting with the world around us.

Communication keeps changing as time marches on. Today, we can send texts over smartphones and we have social media sites and apps that make it both easier and more complicated to connect with others. It's important to remember that it can be tough to really get a feel for what someone's trying to express when all you have is a short message or post with little **context**. Still, people keep adapting to new ways to communicate. What do you think will be next?

It can be hard to tell tone from a text message, email, or a social media post. If you're not sure, ask the person who wrote it!

GLOSSARY

accent (AK-sent) A way of pronouncing words that differs in people from different areas or countries.

articulate (ahr-TIH-kyuh-layt) To express something or show feeling through words.

complicated (KAHM-pluh-kay-tuhd) Hard to explain or understand; with many parts.

context (KAHN-tekst) The situation in which something happens.

contradict (kahn-truh-DIKT) To say or do the opposite of something.

conversation (kahn-vuhr-SAY-shuhn) A talk involving two people or a group of people.

distracted (dis-STRAK-tuhd) Having attention drawn away.

expression (ik-SPREH-shun) The look on someone's face that shows how they're feeling.

grammar (GRAA-muhr) The rules that explain how words are used in a language.

hone (HOHN) To practice something, such as a skill or strength, to get better at that activity.

influence (IN-floo-uhns) An effect one thing has on another.

information (in-fuhr-MAY-shuhn) Knowledge or facts about something.

slang (SLANG) Words that are not considered part of a standard language and are used informally.

summarize (SUH-muh-riiz) To tell information again using fewer words.

verbal (VUHR-buhl) Having to do with words; spoken instead of written.

INDEX

A
accent, 8
Alex (gray parrot), 6
American Sign Language (ASL), 8
animals, 7

B
body language, 10. 22
British Sign Language (BSL), 8

C
context, 22

E
emotions, 22
expression, 10
eye contact, 12, 20

F
feelings, 4, 6, 10

G
grammar, 8, 14
Green, John, 20

L
languages, 8

M
Marshall, John, 17
Matlin, Marlee, 8
message, 4, 11, 22

P
Pepperberg, Irene, 6
practice, 18, 20, 22

Q
questions, 5, 16, 19

S
slang, 14
social media, 4, 22

T
texts, 22

W
words, 4, 7, 8, 10, 14, 20
writing, 4, 8, 20

PRIMARY SOURCE LIST

Page 9
Marlee Matlin and her star on the Hollywood Walk of Fame in Hollywood, California. Photograph. May 6, 2009.

Page 17
John Marshall, fourth chief justice of the U.S. Supreme Court. Painting. ca. 1810. Cephas Thompson.

Page 21
John Green at the *Paper Towns* premiere in New York City. Photograph. July 21, 2015. Jim Spellman.

WEBSITES

Due to the changing nature of Internet links, PowerKids Press has developed an online list of websites related to the subject of this book. This site is updated regularly. Please use this link to access the list: www.powerkidslinks.com/SSEL/communication